Implexures

Karen Mac Cormack

Chax Press and West House Books

Because of its multi-national nature this book contains an intentional mix of North American and UK spellings and usage.

The author thanks both the Canada Council for the Arts and the Toronto Arts Council for grants towards this work in 2000 and 2001 respectively.

Thanks also to the editors and publishers who published sections from *Implexures* in *The Gig, On Word,* and in chap-book form, housepress.

Special thanks to Charles Alexander and Alan Halsey.

Supported by Tucson Pima Arts Council and by the Arizona Commission on the Arts with funding from the State of Arizona and the National Endowment for the Arts.

ISBN for Chax Press 0-925904-42-2
ISBN for West House Books 1-904052-11-8

Chax Press / 101 W. Sixth St., no. 6 / Tucson, Arizona 85701 / USA
West House Books / 40 Crescent Road / Nether Edge, Sheffield S7 1HN / UK

*This ongoing text is dedicated with love
to those (living and deceased) who form
my community, creative and personal.*

Time tangled; it never ran in a straight scythe cut, as they pretended in the moralities, but lay in loops, like the grass at haying time when the conies scampered for safety, and stem and flower were upside down together. — Bryher *(The Player's Boy)*

One

historical letters 1
Sunday was a definite break-away into Difference. — Susan Hicks Beach (née
Christian) to Jacques Derrida circa 1880

Saturday afternoon: a colonial country's thunderstorm, the origins of this fire could
almost rival Malta, winter somewhere between a famous neighbour in the last
century and "an elasticity of spirits" out to Ceylon. One refers to birth through
paper — a certificate, photographs, celluloid, (now) the VCR and DVD. The
starting point is not realized by a new addition as centres are grown from collisions.
Vegetation and climate are remarked upon but their letters they destroyed in
ensuing years and less heat. The performance occupied several days.

Molecules might not have been as confused as I thought probable, the two from the
northern hemisphere less seven and a return to places in it for all three within half
those years. The dog was quarantined. So to Saxon *Doom* from Norse *Lag* always
defying definition as many marriages attest. Elsewhere (the word emblematic of my
vocabulary) other photographs were taken, letters direct us to "Mc or Mac" no
longer prefixed island surnames. In the Sudan the Anwar Dam covers the spot
exactly (planes had propellers then) and figs greeted us to so many palms.

The disappointments of a generation skewed by cynicism or performance mean the
wars inhabit some individuals on an ongoing basis and not only those of the 21st
century. Cousins married each other more often than not, an act perhaps "devastating
to humour." Recognize the ache for what it is, reside there, not knowing opinions,
hear a rosary of sunsets with the bells. Disowned as much for himself as her English

one. (One false step beyond the Cliffs of Moher into the fog and so to sea.)
Others were swimming in the lake before I could. One manoeuvre too many and algae came into view, there were bubbles under the water eyes OPEN for this other world. I didn't even choke they were so prompt in rescue and (later) censure. Wraparound marginless concern and more driftwood. A child faces a first remembered nightmare falling from a suspension bridge in the French car, two parents in the front seat the Pacific joins us.

She who burnt the archives married only after her parents death(s), but it was still an unfortunate date. Another sister lived apart from the unspeaking husband at the other end of the house. But Henry's every hour is understandable. He went to sea under the windows of home became merchant ships the world over, not a finger's space between them. Map of Africa above the library fireplace.

For these are the characters — sense of direction, observed movements, "time of our lives." The tableaux run through themselves. To absorb a history of family through the centuries requires a forebear's attention to facts and no fear of paper. Remember this. The nights are a time of chosen light, days an elaborate grafting.

Pick a childhood to look at. This doesn't have to be your own, but if it is, the strangeness of certain events may shift unexpectedly. The more central regions are established before questions reach those limits. Corn silk, ridge down a dog's back and sky belong to this imbalance, or the branches of a sailing ship, warp of uniform against young skin, lemons. Smell and taste issue the fissure. In a warmer climate more colour in a covering, less material on the surface. View's residue adheres to memory (as such). Limbs grow, or should, if not pain, but that also gathers in illness and beyond the door's arithmetic, spoken word to page aloud, a number and its half, an apple's seasonal red fades against cover to cover rote. To be made aware of difference, real or in so much, perceived, limits all but anxiety. The volume attunes the song. Will you hear? A promotion to meaning enlists words. This combination reflects selectivity. The romp is a tie to early pleasure. First remembered bite flows there. Mango and frangipani in the garden, followed by papaya — so brief, no smells are registered and came to be appreciated "as if for the first time" years later. *It is a lovely house with an amazing garden full of papaya trees, flowers, bean stalks, peanuts, pens with pigs, rabbits & chickens, a fresh water stream, 2 dogs & a cat. (Castries, Saint Lucia, 1 January 74)*

We pay attention to what we can make sense of, not necessarily all at once, but contemplation and deduction aren't favoured by the very young. Moments are a category we give over to. Sometimes patience delivers more time only for itself. This is unimportant. A life lasts for however long its measured events take place and not all of each registers fully but the fact of evidence lists partially. Spinning doesn't stop, perception changes.

Two

historical letters 2
Desire knows no time but the present. — Aphra Behn
The present is always insatiable because it never exists.— Charles Bernstein

Within the orbit, a pick, a path and much tracasserie. At first, entangled leads to more so notches ride the space before the eyes. Enliven the odds. Reduce the party and its funds. Distinguish between examples.

Pneumonia in Mexico, the train's airconditioning a stiff adjustment to the heat on either side and under the wheels. In San Miguel de Allende there was cough mixture with chloroform and sleep came and went but the dreams were always there. Many descriptions of landscapes, city and town squares, turquoise against thin altitudes in contrast to the bloodstones of youth, *agua potabile*, the rain but not the tropics. Maps augment possibilities, shift decisions, and co-exist with timetables' fascination.

For a Victorian not prudish on the page, having made mention, she remained discreet, disagreeing (it would seem) with a forebear's tenet that "few of one's secrets are worth keeping to oneself." Falling portraits woke her in the night but possibility of an intruding danger occurred only after her facts were re-positioned. That we might view ourselves across the century in anything other than static form, introduce a working draft to clearer scrutiny, steal in the pen to library's likeness engrave . . . this is not a conversation nor a theme, it is a letter, another fold in a fan where the writer in this decade sees the angled history of a past decade's correspondent snapped shut.

Sometimes the moments move as silk freefalls from head down to knees, or knot stubbornly across the neck. The cufflinks are a puzzle so easy to lose. Any other survival at hand and just as much yours as mine. Opinion contrives originality and that is *not* forthcoming. Loosen the limerick just so, address translation to *poste restante* and the *billets* might be *doux*. Desire isn't an endorsement or not of character, it's what hasn't gone away when you (both) wake up.

Declensions of travel as in a language, shift. *I also met the former Deputy Minister of the West Indies . . . (well, he said he was the former . . .). We met him in Castries in a restaurant where we had our lunch. He was nice but extremely conceited.* (Castries, Saint Lucia, 17 January 74) What might have been the fastest ship of his day would not be so for us, but the observed speed of a bird's flight is more or less the same for both. Fireworks go differently, though if only the art of piano tuning could be seen and not heard. The imprints seep away to layers of another's memory and other after that. Clothes and customs and superstitions change, attitudes to sex and what is or isn't "magic," but the seeking of fortune is with us, political machination omnipresent, "endangering" itself is a way of living. Across the heartline studs can't stick.

Three

historical letters 3

Is? I mean was. *But then, I mean also* will be. *And so I cleave to the nostalgic present, as grammarians might call it.* — Max Beerbohm

The pier's better known through its many images in films. Songs on and off the radio drift into hearing up and down day or night. A hand reaches for another's fingers. There are many reasons for wearing gloves, temperature the least of them. Is it at one's side front and centre back and forth? Salt air and creaking, a stone beach, not sand. The wind picks up, but not necessarily in the same place. Hard Knot Pass in the rain one is easily convinced of as permanently cold if not always wet. Not so the *Meltame* in Naxos, where white blisters blue noon heat, the jelly fish's sting scars for half a year, ouzo distends nocturnal notes (the music is *always* loud). Chalk as a colour not a taste. The mosaic is splashed to shimmering in the museum . . . water beyond varnish inhabiting movement. Curves of the archway lead to coolness for a rectangular segment of afternoon. Many visual depictions of these islands' architecture veer to abstraction a realist dreams of . . . *on our way home we passed a restaurant, also on the beach, where a band was playing and the Greeks were dancing. We sat down and a Greek man at once bought each of the four of us a beer, (a common practice) and we danced and danced and suddenly Euripides said "We're all going to Melanes" (Alexandra's village) and so we piled into a pickup truck and watched the sun come up over the mountains and appeared at her parents' door at 6 a.m. They were not at all surprised and gave us coffee and then put us to bed and we slept until 1 p.m. and were woken up only to eat a gargantuan dinner which consisted of: goat, spaghetti, salad, bread, cheese, fish, wine, oranges and a yellow-orange fruit, about the size of a small plum, which tasted like passion-fruit but did not have nearly as many seeds. Then we looked at the beautiful view . . . Melanes is a terraced village and from their house you see a deep valley and directly across from you a very lush mountain. The land is completely covered with fruit trees! The quiet was the most striking thing, it was as if the car had never been heard of, (but Alexandra's parents have a huge fridge!)*

These people, this lovely old couple who had welcomed us as if we were their own children, constantly fussed that we had not eaten enough, (I was ready to BURST) and Euripides kept apologizing that no one else spoke English, to which we replied that we were sorry we didn't speak Greek. They were very natural and talked and talked with no inhibition, even had an argument, (it lasted all of three minutes). It was a very special day because not many foreigners are brought into the hearts of the Greeks and we have been especially lucky in this respect. Adonis and "Mama" have adopted us and Alexandra's parents certainly did for the day and would love us to visit again. They are expert cheese-makers (?), which I think is one of their forms of income.

Anyway at 3 p.m. we ran all the way up the street-steps to catch the bus back to Naxos. (Their house is about one third of the way down the mountain, but not at the bottom of the village.) The bus ride back was breathtaking (we were on a road which went up near the top of the mountains and right down into the valleys) . . . (Naxos, Greece, 28 May 76)

Borders as windshields. In Sardinia the "crossroads of death" pushed both into contortion. A poorly marked intersection's preoccupied driver (the car was French). Backseat view of impact more the sound of metal into metal flipping upside down to ground gravel spinning head wedged in rear dashboard three and a half revolutions but no silence. Stop. Voices and sound of running feet approaching. In any language the driver said "I'm sorry." Pushing outwards from distorted immobility. The sensation when lying down that the head is too heavy for the neck to lift from a pillow but no x-rays now or then so shoulder on because the car was a write-off. Our bruises faded even if in Old English (with its gendered nouns) the word for *woman* was neuter, while that for *snake* was feminine.

Four

historical letters 4
Contrary to a tracing, which always returns to the "same," a map has multiple entrances . . . A map is a matter of performance, whereas the tracing always refers to an alleged "competence." — Gilles Deleuze & Felix Guattari

Base treachery in an after-dinner mood labelled national existence. Exclusion from English and European history, now a need for improved trade, "Tenure of the Straw," always freehold — threatened. Jurisdiction between high water mark and distracted tymes indeed conceive candlelight. A 17th century library of "nigh one thousand books." Death is a blend originating in a watch-tower. Storms accounted for her unacquaintance with the fact, then the drawbridge was pulled up. Enough to leave by and no spilled ink.

Now, as if filled with a liquid repeatedly frozen, partially thawed, glacée again and so on sore Sisyphus, one sees the night becoming day dark cracked to dusk again black the vague sense of this as a recurring rhythm for certain schedules. So many words around us, lines joining to break on paper, pause on air. Do not hesitate to compare "relayed fixity" with "no such thing."

Two children, a typewriter in a caravan (or mobile home) and many pieces of paper flying from inky fingers inhabit a grownup's anger. The desire or power to intrigues was a curiosity at odds with parents, movement being easy to come at. The house *did* come down. A French car on the road's season of driftwood, horses, cornfields, the range and measles. Learning to tie one's shoe laces, picking all the flowers in a mother's (newly planted) garden. Sides of beef hanging from hooks. Mountains, too, became curious creatures' haunts en route to town and nautical Punch lands Judy. Bells ringing the lambs in.

Form at certain taverns never documentary during their scramble. To the west spell jeopardy and drop to lower ground rasp's running with a lantern. Later through the front door, down the hall and out again, coach, frills adhere to it. Horn of boxwood and in existence a diary usually is a provoking document. Hovered very much to the fore and exasperating. Consent withheld and why? Every record drawn a blank and so impossible to forgive her being a Perfect Lady. Drifting coming on to the answering mountain has made a picture. Into three editions and many infidelities (the former begot missiles). An independent line . . . freedom of outlook (not one but two bribes of peerage failed) and then the Repeal of the Salt Tax. Meanwhile, diligent in her Latin and "very new-fangled of my Italian," she didn't object to his taking a sprogue now and then. A "nip" appeared in the pit and he was then alone. Trappings beyond perennial drain, the dusk, in his chair, but no marker or tablet, it being December what flowers could there have been?

One of many criss-crosses, stunted trees — no, wheat hazing the horizon, not much in formal religion, definition of "little white lies" insufficient and too many changes in temperature (though none of them markedly southern). We share a lingual experience. Waiting for the pipe smoke to settle in a room full of newspapers. In those days the accents couldn't be accommodated and Lucien Lelong's Number 7 wasn't known by name. Two "exotic" plants, large against the books to these younger children in equal portions, but William "started on the performance of buying them out." Any timepiece will do. Nothing left of either property on his death, everything put up for sale (family portraits, too), this "dreary action . . . already there in Time." A son went off to the Zulu war, made three fortunes and lost them all. Driving cab in London, so as to marry and die in the silver mines of Mexico. *After leaving Chetumal we went to Porto Juarez, where we met some very nice people who spoke a bit of English & invited us to stay at their house overnight. They were young (20s), one of them was an accountant, another was studying architecture & they all want to travel. It's hard for Mexicans to save money because their salaries aren't usually good & unless you are born wealthy, chances are you never will be. There is a very sharp, clear division between rich and poor in this country.* (in transit, Mexico, 12 April 74) There were two daughters. "If only things happened in life as they do in properly constructed novels . . ." she wrote, I read and write again for those who see the ghosts departing.

Unregarded, the advent converted (all over the countryside) the political agent and postmistress. Terraces and dignity to prevail in full blast of shattered went in answer to toughness. Decoratively attired very smiling ever escaped became familiar with time went on.

Five

historical letters 5
With all these elements of navigation at my disposal, I become obsessed with where I am.
— Diane Ward

There are *no* photographs from that summer of white go-go boots, dresses on the rise through and through. The dog had died the year before, a small perfect bird found on the beach encouraged me to free an admired (hostage) butterfly. Its release was as much a will *not* to see the stillness associated with demise. Death isn't so much silence as immobility sunk into the body. There followed a marked interest in bones and so to palaeontology.

Scott meddled once again, this time on the Scottish side of *MacGregor's Gathering*. Robert Louis Stevenson through (in) his claim, too. Along the way there's the inventor of the reflecting microscope, first barometer put together in Scotland and one of them invented a "species of" gatling gun. His octogenarian self had to tolerate Newtonian intervention (an abuse of ingenuity Sir Isaac claimed!). His son (David Gregorie II) was in conflict with Oxford University over reforms and told Pepys about it in letters. ("He took a degree at Balliol, was made Savilian Professor of Astronomy.") Mathematics were *their* forte. To compliment memory, learning poems proved my part, these became "more." One (another) move resulted in (temporary) loss of multiplication. Conformity's precedence over ability plus knowledge. The calculator proves it. I came to Chaucer late in the tales and don't divide words' appearance. What's a good logarithm to gerund? All those quiet petals become part of the wallpaper as they wilt, but not that illegitimate daughter alive at one hundred, left all the property.

Elegance "had something to do with carriage, a little with gesture, a little with the management of skirts. It was not the same thing as stateliness." Nor a crossing on a ship. Chronology doesn't improve immediacy. The dolphins alongside are there with someone else now. Triggers for touching but be steady, weight and balance, ensure. From the cotton fields spun wealth but the Civil War cut that thread. What is meaning at the side of the road if not a confirmation of direction, right or wrong? At sea the compass and sextant keep this in hand. His extravagant tastes matched his daring and so he ran the blockade . . . he was in New York well before most other forebears *because* his luck ran out.

One of them went to Japan and India and brought cricket to the Isle of Man. He travelled afar repeatedly and his published research was exhaustive, if deficient in "technique." Beaches (surprisingly at this stage?) sift in memory rock to sand, pebble, volcanic black, shingle grey, more numerous than absent, (or how to perplex a leitmotif). One walks on them (avoiding medical waste), swims from them (still), consults water level versus erosion and builds accordingly if possible. An example's brevity marks the tide. "Now" there's another country a few minutes away by ferry. Hours and days for other nations' islands. The particular salt air we carry around an ocean. Resting on banks with interest. Politics run more than two by two and moments of heat thicket a blanket's wool. Never a glance of single word at the time.

After Baden-Baden (another fortune-not-yet-made?) a small Georgian house and "before the next summer was over" she was born, but no day of the week is given. "From now on the tiresome first person singular will have to be brought into use."

Six

historical letters 6

The unnatural *has always given people pleasure. Ring through the nose, hairstyling, makeup in the hollows of the eyes, Rococo, etc. — and today, lips.*
— Robert Musil (*Notebook 31*: 7 Feb 1930–Spring 1936)

The word *glamour* "developed" as the Scottish spelling of the English *gramayre* or *gramarye* (entered into English in the 14th century denoting grammar or learning) but by the 15th century it signified occult learning. By the close of that century (in its modern spelling) *glamour* meant a specific form of magic spell or charm cast by devils through the agency of (usually) female witches, and supposedly caused the illusory disappearance of the penis. Your *Vogue* or mine? Meanwhile the first (English) fashion plate was published in *The Lady's Magazine* in 1759.

The Clans' intolerance of others' actions speaking louder than words: diminishment all round. Unable to use their own name, such tactics left shadows and one in particular carried himself "too proudlie" in "these dangerous and distracted tymes." Nothing original in the passions driven overseas the greatest obstacle open menace. "Cark, dole and drule." The island from and to and fro.

"The habit of being ahead in conception always marks a man as 'dangerous' in regulated communities." High ceilings, sustained cold the fireplaces could not correct to temperate, this way the given goes diurnal. The deaths accumulate, conditions faced, dispersed, tributes written in the far away as "home" so centuries crease.

A "foothill" town, really . . . *the only other person on board is an American friend of theirs who used to be part of the Apollo Space Program but decided he liked boats better . . . Power boats are ugly on the outside but quite luxurious inside. There is far more space due to the three levels, or decks, & hot water, (that's a change) & the boat even has stabilizers for a smoother ride, so, all in all, it's more comfortable but not as much fun . . . Last night we arrived at the Marina in Cozumel, an island just off the coast of the Yucatan. The largest town is San Miguel where we will catch a ferry to the mainland . . . I had venison for the first time.* (Cozumel, Mexico, 30 March 74) Having weathered the storms the Caribbean offered this curved fact of moving up a long country from east of, northwest was a pleasure and surprise (thus including pneumonia). Holes in both thumbs, the eventual visit to a hospital's language challenge ultimately left scars. This is the faraway those living in a cold climate vacation to. Senses of time are learned, not inherited, appropriated, or open for negotiation. Pacing oneself is first an acknowledgement of when weakness sets in. (The feel of a taffeta as opposed to a velvet alibi. Knife's the same.) Opening and closing the eyes on a moving landscape is often described as "dream-like," but instead is closer to the relative. Daily passage in a vehicle obscures what happens to a building. Let several months pass and its changed colour and deepening (or even repaired) cracks are more obvious. The tendency is to compare what follows to what was first scene, hence Athens reminded an overheard Australian of the Greek section she knew in Melbourne. . . .

Cold sometimes at six thousand feet, dust and silver through fingers learning the acetylene torch. Lighting the furnace to heat water reduced eyelashes to "love." The eyes wandered. Wind blew pages of early poetry further up the hill (before or after piñatas?). *Saw a magnificent Aztec dance show. Approximately 50 descendants dressed up in beautifully vivid costumes with gigantic dyed-feather headdresses & shoes with*

bells on them performed in the square. This fiesta commemorates San Miguel Day.
(San Miguel de Allende, Mexico, 28 September 74) He went for the silver mines and
two daughters of which no more mention was made.

The case in itself is leather. Lined with a "watered" fabric to resemble silk, the
compartments' size conforms to an earlier era's more commodious requirements.
This business of having too little income constrains (overtly and otherwise) view to
the self occluded. Nothing new in that in *any* age. Into this would go the jars of
lotions, ointments, powders and rouge essential to maintaining the face while
travelling. Combs suggest elaborate length (before spray gel). There is a faint smell
of talc still associated with her bending her "grandmother's" head toward "me"
when I was a child. A photograph, which is particularly attentive to her awareness of
senses other than sight, also comes to bear on the collection of images of the
woman for whom this case was made. It offers no secrets but the talc's maker
remains unknown. The case is, at this time, not "untouched" but cared for, intact.
So many other items have been bruised in the 20th century.

Tarmac where rain recently stopped falling. Thin end of lollipop falls from a child's
hand. If it's not night it doesn't matter (but on this run it's usual for arrival). Knock
on the door. A man's shoulders. Cotton or wool. Bombs in the city's "elsewhere."
Candle flame. Recorded music. Casino ignored around the corner. Sitting at the
table in the downstairs kitchen. Glasses, bottles, smoke and other additives, GMT
blues. Any day of the week except the 29th. To handle an antique may or may not
encourage pause, but this everyday item was one of the last objects held before he
died. Not what this does but *how* it is . . . these troublesome entries before the
unknown. The fact of death is foreseeable, a given, but timing is anything,
whenever.

A lineage of those who live beyond . . . their means, our times. The setting itself is broken, not simply quaint, or out of place in present context — it cannot hold what was intended for it. We do not move any closer to each other. There are boundaries and actions to go with them, and sometimes the weather products intervene. An image pertains to what is imagined, not seen, but there are (literally) those who would change that.

The sheets were blue by what the streetlight outside the window provided. Other rooms in that house were cold, despite whiskey, gin, various recordings of Callas, Costello. Pitted streets deviated at the front door, vectors arrived at surface one. Through the years of twists and numerous preoccupations the folds eventually converged and so from profiles to full frontal view the angles curved to meet. Intensity's understatement. An overlay of rain, June sunshine, bombs.

Sun on the deck, through the trees, in leaves scattered by the bucket and cloth. Light working on and through the water (no playing here). Grapefruit at hand, fingers on rail feel brass. (Which century is this description closest to?) Air strips porpoising. Tropical month, or no, track-while-scan. The water's beyond through-light lapping. Metallic in mouth and eye, this surface event's all ripple, on and off frame by framed, legless. Inch of glass between us (centimetres say so). Epaulettes in the heat-grown-accustomed-to, someone else's hand seen to . . . *visit* is a word brought out too often. *When I tell people down here about snow & Canadian winter temperatures a look of disbelief crosses their faces. I can understand why, too. If I had never felt anything below 65° or 70° (F) I'd find it hard to imagine as well.* (Castries, Saint Lucia, 17 January 74)

Flesh carved, flesh stitched, operations doctors live by to this or any other day (saved him?). Elide to fruitfulness rather than purpose these reminiscences, a stronger motion than liqueur or capsule rides on. Reviews sever favour from fiction. The chair was purchased in Los Angeles, folded into transability with cardboard and now rocks gently under a more northern moon, keening west(ward). Small rugs are easier to relocate (so the caravan tents were sumptuous from the sand up every night). China breaks silk's silence. A handful, no more, to sigh on the stars clear night's breathless, amplify blink.

"The old moon in the new moon's arms." Canister or canopy or an eye to the backroom, women are instructed not to frown from infancy up. Flat afternoons indicate edge of residency. Falling off or on targets what isn't in the circle.

There are place names of winding incomprehension, the curves of an unlearned alphabet, but the politics being what they are, shoulders and arms are covered and remain so for the duration. A walk can go for a long way, but to cross a desert must mean to zigzag. Was it Tenerife for you, too? But the camels are in Lanzerote. Heat streaks through the afternoon the bird sang to that morning, where a church was so dark the smell of cut flowers replaced sight.

An even hum to practise makes practice not perfection or perfection. We speak into microphones and questions come later. We both went to Puerto de la Cruz, skirts of varying lengths above puddles, on bar stools, absent in camera, address of a kind. Hunger as an invasion or contraction? Doing without luxury as the name implies divided categories, *inarrugable* (crease-resisting), inarguable. How long will it take to anything else? This isn't mine. Go back to straight ahead. The timing is wrong per person. A visitor's function is to spend money, whether or not the economy's local prostitutes are down by the water tying their laces to head over heels. I want to hire the charge per hour. That mirror fits very well. Can this be invisibly mended? Do not bend per word, reverse the charges out of gas. "Months (like days) are masculine in gender and do not require a capital letter." How dangerous that cobra looks by my watch! Don't talk about yourself unless you know how to dance. Everybody wants to punch a time clock with shorter hours and higher pay. Perhaps you would like to rent that cheque? No one can predict exactly all along the track were scattered the salesman's samples. What may happen in the future was killed instantly. At Boston instead of money below the bridge inside the box out of anger. Since reason as soon as whether until what time on the other hand, when? A swarm of bees (*un enjambre de abejas*) not a staff of clerks (*un cuerpo de clérigos*) so tired of sleeping tried something else.

The hands are full, mouth empty, mind on the road, body outstretched to enable disclosure the inside on the outside's screen with dye clear until x-ray's capacity. Audience of two and equipment past Remembrance Day's horizon extended all the way to each. Possibility's not half of any binary so it's every system to itself and. The earth, no beginnings, no ends, sum of every. Movement as a *place* itself so no motion is homeless.

Seven

historical letters 7
*I only stayed with her once at Quenington & she tired easily in any case wasn't that
interested in relations until her book came out.* — Margaret Mac Cormack
(née Ward Thomas)

Plaw's most famous design was for one of the houses where she lived (circular) but
now (un-phoenix-like) it has burned to the ground. Is it ever not-raining on the
planet? Instructions lose themselves in comprehension. The fan's folded pleats
touch both ends of the centuries his actions span, and expansive, spread. The
photograph shows him aboard ship, the pose an official holiday recording, stiff with
polished shoes and crossed legs, wool the cloth of abundance. *One of the problems
with beginning one's travelling at such a young age is that one quickly loses the desire to
"rough" it. Indeed, I wonder if I ever HAD it!!!???* (Carrara, Italy, 27 May 78)

We, the descendants newly-met, sit discussing his controlled bequest, wishing the
photographed man capable of contemporary speech. Instead, the cavalier spaniels
provide background noise, one of them snoring through references to other deaths,
another shifting from lap to lap. My relative is the same age as my father would be
now. Ripples in a century the eyes blink a tear forms. This house stands astride two
parishes, the boundary running through the entrance porch. It was in the staircase
tower that Elizabeth watched the hawking in the "faire parkes" from a single room,
but it was in the "withdrawing chamber" that she gave her answer to the envoy of
the Duke of Anjou in 1578, regarding his proposal of marriage. (He died in 1584,
unsuccessful to the end.) On her first visit in 1571 she heard of the Duke of
Norfolk's complicity in the Ridolphi plot. Lunch in the oldest part of the house
(circa 1470) where in the south dining room one looks at a knife and fork set

"recovered from the baggage train of prince Charles Edward after the battle of Culloden," as my cousin wrote in his "short history" of Horham Hall. The gardens are full of ghost roses and the dogs emerge happily wet from grass too-well-acquainted with rain. There are hugs and kisses before the train, a sense of looking at each other more quizzically than is customary, given the newness of seeing a relative never-met-before in so many decades, the intensity of learning about another's lifetime over a few hours, distance arrived at, arrival no longer distant.

Black suit, back in the hub, back and forth between the OSO and passport office (a difference of chemicals placed me in the photo booth) missing only a hat. Security measures were BLACK ALERT and the visitor's pass didn't attach readily to my lapel. The ceremony of instruction and receipt over, turning south on Chancery Lane a cool summer day as far as the body could be taken through to the fan with a flick opened wide and on every moment was assured "opportunity." My breathing in the world expanded.

His day must have involved a desk, different pens for numerous decisions, an array of assistants, and a suitably enthusiastic (impressed) greeting from members of the household at the end of the day. The watercolour shows a large house set in copious garden and grounds. Distracted by another watercolour and an appreciation of Soane's exquisite sense of space within his passion for collecting. The open fragility of chair backs and legs compared with the solidity of successive bookcases strikes a balance not interrupted by family breakfasting.

In turning to letters I discover he was called Peter by his daughter, who, " . . . if I was going away soon after it [breakfast] [I] would not partake at all which Peter always called being "Journey Proud" — a weird expression I don't know if it originated in Yorks." [12 Dec 1966]

She seldom if ever inserted a comma and her periods were dashes on the page. Sentences in paragraphs were often totally unrelated. With item 357 the sale ended with "A large heap of assorted timber." An example of Margaret's paragraph:

Pink was 24 in June when she married 1893 & her birthday was Nov. 17th
so she was 25 in 1893 & I'll let you work out her birth year. Chol has
had the most awful hair clip only very few short hairs left on his head.
[14 Dec 1966]

A terrace, palm trees, ivy, and views of both mountains and sea at this point the sun is closer to the latter's reflected pink. Sometimes *aperitivi* appear in fair weather for an hour or so. It's not the chill of the glass that melts small distances though they slide more easily down our throats with a swallow or two. Jasmine in the darkening air lifted by a breeze sinks to one's pillow inside the bedroom. Hills and high heels everywhere. The cypress(es) juxtapose clouds. Visual residue of centuries becomes a chosen route in town where every *caffé* attracts political affiliations (the best pastries are served in conservative premises so morning coffee is consumed alone more often than not).

When J & I went to Milano a couple of weeks ago, to go to a major Canadian
exhibition (sculpture, video, et al) & to meet Bernard Tanzi, owner of this house, they
had dinner with the family & the following came to light. This house was built in 1560
(has remained in Tanzi hands all these centuries!), was badly bombed by the Germans
in WWII, hence the fragment of a painting, etc. (Did I already mention this?)
Anyway, in the enclosed photo you see the kitchen windows (barred) & the shuttered
windows belonging to what is now my study. Past the green bush on the left hand side
are the windows of our bedroom (not visible). Isn't the marble bathtub on my left,

great? And as for me, I'm wearing the black jacket you gave me & holding a cup of tea while trying for a brainwave. (Carrara, Italy, 10 May 79 [?])

33

34

The railway up and down the coast and inland to Firenze leaves behind the marble dust, compressors, diamond disks, mountains. A season of flat shoes emerges in a city where one's grammar and pronunciation are corrected when seeking information in the *stazione*, though it's to Perugia that seekers-of-the-most-desired accent go to school. She went to Italy but did her brother-in-law, on or off shipboard, Ernest? If so, Cinque Terre would have been accessible only by sea or train, no roads were built until long after "my" first visit.

In this act the surfaces touch intermittently and what we refer to as memory lacks the multiplicity of the present though details remain in focussed amplification. Research doesn't "lead" to anything other than more reasons to/for research. The so-called facts give way to correspondence (one-sided in these instances). In thinking about the writing of letters that lingering self-consciousness is least apparent in the recording of family events, distant more often than near. The sunrise in Naxos, the sunsets in Mexico: these are in the same decade but the rainbows at Bolton Abbey come later. (Chronology is the death of us.) *When* we experience an event is only important to the individual whereas *if* and with what results the experience has occurred is of concern to a collective. The family goes in so many directions as to render the singular forever invalid. For Proust it was the *madeleine* rather than the smell of woodsmoke in sight of Tuscan cypresses, or the cool touch of marble even in summer heat. Water in a fountain smelling only of orange blossoms at the end of the day but not the beginning of night. Silk at any moment. Height.

By the end of his letters he was too tired for the past. My Irish grandfather consistently misspelled "carachter" for "character." In the 17th and 18th centuries (in England) the only household article men were more likely to own than women was a clock.

The gold watch belonged to Peter's Mother. I was always intrigued by the fact
that it had a man's-like chain with it but I was always told it was hers . . .
I am pretty sure small watches for females were not made in those days —
whether it belonged to a man originally I don't know. [12 December 1966]

The words unravel, re-form and on the page refer to their meanings sometimes lift
but nothing is settled. To query another age is not to solve a detective novel. Few
questions can be answered as neatly as "yes" or "no." Journeys are not for resting
places move on (to paraphrase). He wrote "I expect my grandfather remembered
the famine but I never heard him talk about it" [23 Sept 70]. Earlier [30 Oct 69]
" . . . but static warfare such as 1914–18 was simply a question of cannon-fodder &
munitions & using both to the full. Hence 14–18 produced no good generals." He
started Latin when he was seven and met my great-grandmother once only in 1918.

I'll tell you about the massive piece of metal . . . The first he knew of it was
(he was wounded on the 5th July 1915 about 5.30 a.m.) when his clothes
were returned to him in his kit bag about Oct. or Nov. 1915 & among the stuff
was a pair of boots he'd been wearing that a.m. & inbedded in the sole & west
of the right boot was that lump of metal. He wrote & enquired from his fellow
warriors how it had got there & they said when they picked him up they found
it inbedded in the boot. It's part of a shell casing. Very lucky he didn't have his
foot blown off, & he kept it as a memento. [20 Dec 1966]

The letter to another cousin is returned with the affixed label stating that "the
addressee has gone away."

Eight

historical letters 8
I expect all those sort of things of hers went to a cousin or a great nephew or great great.
I am not at all sure but think his name was John Christian & have no idea where he
lives. — Margaret Mac Cormack (née Ward Thomas)

The wind as confluence of surfaces tangled if unseen by any "poetress."

Henry served on the *Wolverine* suppressing the slave trade on the East Coast of
Africa (1849–52). "In one's arms" a location of intimacy, though "it is not possible
to be lucid about the dances of society in the interval after the minuet and gavotte
. . . and before the waltz and quadrille."

When that ties what this, a schism, the glimpse of shape of hand inherited line of
neck an eye on both. All the Sunday afternoons of a lifetime. Walk away. *I have, as I*
mentioned earlier, no intention of giving "the family" the details of my lifestyle and
accordingly I should expect envy, to a certain degree. (However, it would appear that
envy has no degrees, a fact I constantly forget. But the implications I read into her letter
cut a little deeper than usual. . . .) (Carrara, Italy, 27 February 78)

In a locale (or at a "location") where seagulls prove nocturnal (the white gulls of
Porto) the Atlantic is a stretch into Baroque sky's cathedral identification. The
steepness rewinds streets to shore, bridges and liquids splay across breeze the
laundry being so copious blocks. She notes that "Even the most scintillating pen can
descend to depths of abysmal boredom when it describes travels." Yet another's
"discretion with her pen is forever a smokescreen." The pages remain sheets of

discrete opacity words are aligned on but while meaning rotates each reader of meanings part attention gaps. "Everybody looked magnificent, nobody happy."

The planet's spinning and our traversing (with) it a shorthand of applied relocation. Never far from near(by). Open-air sex the scent of night grass and line of bark breaking across other than spoke. How the leaves moved post-indentation's "we." Summer night it was the moss-scent fingers slid toward an appreciation of green in multiple shades. A small park off a residential street's still there, though what were once one-hundred-year-old apple trees have been cleared for a motorway. To have gone away again means I've still not met him. Remind the shell of the land sea uncovers, hold the glass up to the eclipse's fifteen minutes.

The windows open out, in, up, or not at all, on a garden, the street, the sea, a lake, river or desert, cobbled courtyard, mountains, sometimes hills, with or without curtains, a highway, motorway, freeway, other windows' occupants, deck. Cicada time in the present but Jezebel's famous for learning censure by simply looking out.

From a prior car a winter afternoon's snow on the road and in fields passed by on time for coach home. The oncoming pick-up right in the middle it's a good thing there weren't seatbelts fastened as the swerve up the incline rolled us into the back seats upside down over the side of the then empty road. No injuries except to the car in dimpse (twilight). Three strikes and light's out.

Nine

historical letters 9
. . . the story of my sleeping in a haunted room . — Margaret Mac Cormack

November grey-cloud dawn or slightly after the other child asleep in her bed across
the room not her gaze responsible for waking a chill specifically emanating from
foot of bed covers intact no open window to account for equally grey outline
containing haze of figure features indistinct approaching but then a halt sensing
(seemingly) a child's astonishment combined with fear literally pinching oneself
awake as this presence did not make sense I was six and a half years old and though
there didn't appear to be hostility involved the fear won out the male figure
remained at the foot of the bed for some time (probably minutes though the
impression has lasted this lifetime as eternity) gradually fading and in so doing the
air around the bed returned to customary "morning" temperature but there's no
recollection of a return to sleep.

If perplexed then how many sways to purpose, Babylon, or no examples of (her)
father's handwriting? Easily misglozed (misinterpreted) the missives she sent
implied an expression meaning to express regret. Icicles fuse alarmingly during the
middle of a month severe in days when the sky is either white instead of, or pale
with crystals falling around streetlights in the dark. Approximations divide
information's multiples so shadow data arise. The apportioning of information
causes facts to re-form as "versions" (there's no such creature as a "home truth" in
this life). What a text leaks resistance to joins. Even if a number is taken the machine
won't serve at margin before *or* best date's from. As a reference the event was a
reading but the year before's a ceremony it was a snowy day so the hat was in its box
the recorded music started and stopped the flush came and stayed.

39
è&

How to enter the concept of "re" not as a graft but to experience nuance (shape of the *qui*). What is left is nothing more left to do except removal. We know beyond price what isn't emptiness won't lack for anything else resumes habit.

The sound of the splash louder than duck. Looking into the River Lee a man's face responded "swimming" already transposed by current and another man running with buoy along quay to help. Sound of two fire trucks approaching from the other side and two policemen on this standing next to their motorcycles before poets as spectators to hyperthermia to each other to the rescue.

From a Rathmines morning to Trinity night the spaces between the voicing of words all of it rain reigning by castle the concealed object in hand and nothing but shot for "the British" his gun was illusory his disturbance real. "Not all Irish people are like that" said the woman who directed me to the entrance. A refrain of "right name wrong accent" in gaze when hearing speech open your anecdote and it's not "fine," *be* "grand." Cheek by trial by whiskey by language by name bifurcation but by saying dust off inner "depths."

When an angle becomes an encumbrance for lack of other settings take a viewpoint for the walk. A remembered use is different from a newly discovered one. The parley of exhaustion or the hunt is downed out of site.

More bridges, longer daylight hours to walk along and among. To enclose an approach is arch. The stairs are noticeable up to the fifth floor, less so to the ground. Watching a white cat "playing" with a white butterfly as a form of symmetry or even monotone. Contract as a word not so many words release.

The steaminess of the air summer heat and thousands slowly entering an arena for a concert satin trousers rain-jacket adhering to skin the acoustics weren't meant for *Jumping Jack Flash* in the dark smell of fluids trickling lipstick option passage concrete intensity no encore because one of them fainted and the configuration ends in disappointment and further showers home with a tear in the fabric the lights inside and out darkness glossy pavements several stories down sixteenth summer listening to *Exile* a certain criticism but then so many stars had died so the point was not to complain too soon. Sunday mornings proved the worst stretch grey wasn't limited to one side of the pane serious attention to each gradation at such intervals the body's largest organ isn't skin but contraction and expansion of emotion.

That same summer (?) the bar with stuffed birds in cages high above the tables hence dusty (not a pre-asthma concern) perennially dark and now torn down or converted by some fast-food chain but then with make-up and never jeans always high heels we would enter by not looking around talking to each other about whose poetry we were reading sitting carefully at one of those small tables (were they round?) and we would successfully order beer under age there was music the ageing queens ignored us we were learning the art of being in a bar no threat of male proposition (that wasn't part of "the point") two friends (still friends) on disco summer nights in from the heat. Once the bartender appeared with two bottles (not ordered) to our surprise the man in the corner had bought us these drinks (he wore a hat?) and we sighed looking at each other and towards him cautiously raised our glasses as he made no move to join us (to our relief) he watched not stirring and we returned to our conversation I occasionally glanced in his direction I formed no clear recollection of him his age or inclination in the *Parkside* she went to proms, I did not.

Reshuffle. Splay. Both hands know what (where) the heart is thinking. All periods end in pieces. Wingtips, no visible rings but a buttonhole's for the rose. Sanctuary as hours without rather than in. It's not that you're silent it's the unfamiliarity of communicating that makes exchanges intermittent.

What would parentheses add to a partial understanding of parental/filial estrangement? The separation's ongoing insofar as remembered trust is an underlay to acknowledged distress (or separation that knows no elasticity chips forward). There are no queues for listening to a disintegration, but the mismatch continues (a form of overtime).

Word product on every shelf and airwave redefining *mobile* as so many public cubicles invisible but tight to the huddle, arrive. Suddenly the act of writing a private letter connotes increased intimacy. Words are also perishable, though not in the same breath. To be dealt a hand or given a lead, the match is made to be ignited.

Ten

Events are, after all, only things that happen untimely and out of place; one is as it were, mislaid or forgotten, and one is as helpless as an object that nobody bothers to pick up. — Robert Musil *(Tonka)*

The fires and what we have in them irons aside. A seventeen-year-old writes *I was just woken by your telegram, it terrified me . . . answered the phone . . . I thought somebody had died or something equally upsetting.* (Castries, Saint Lucia, 3 February 74)

How much information does *information* require for the dispersal of a combination (of)? Many "I"s have travelled, to be moved left, right, off . . . any map. A recognition is the beginning of an ability for tracking (nanosecond by portion). I "see myself" as recognizable in correspondence posted half a life-time-ago and then there was a working towards some of what exists "now." But *how* one knows is equally crucial to *what* one knows in the inseparable *when. Where* is the locator.

I remember years *ago one of Peter's sisters went for a trip to the West Indies & brought back a jar of Guava jelly & for ages after that Pink tried to get more but I suppose in those days it was not imported.* [3 Feb 1967]

For some it will always be easier to apologize (again) instead of remembering before the act (again) that requires/necessitates the apology, despite "assurances" that such behaviour won't manifest "in future." Moisture is not a tear.

What any environment is described by or acts through — language, so even the motions of a dancer's feet make contact with the words *floor, air, cleaving.* In ballet, to "correct" hyper-extended arms requires an unaccustomed utilisation of muscles, similar to the mechanisms, musculatory and otherwise in "the performance of the game called Society."

That lifting of a finger or the space a breath negotiates and it's deflation — what's the matter *is* the matter — when randomness becomes specific, common even, so it's not with relief this trigger set the door ajar another disappearance registers something more — left out.

Just as atoms move even in stillness the body isn't static . . . death, too, as process. If we could perceive all the *invisibles* all of the time we might re-think the notion of space. What is termed the present is a site, blank in the mo(ve)ment one blinks, process (again), so what constitutes the distance we leave (is it behind us, or stepped away from moment by moment to become years or cultural shift?).

Palmerston Gardens, Dublin. Due south of Belgrave Square down Belgrave (Road?), which becomes Palmerston Road and if one turns west along Cowper Road one arrives at Palmerston Gardens, a north/south street. (When *finis* becomes *finish* and gaelic is absent?)

I write myself "out" not of ideas but of the engagement we review with criticism . . . a swivel, a questioning, hours in the twenty-four can't manage or mirage, would *we* to *I* that? Is this even vaguely similar to the disenchantment with the touchstone (now estranged from), that country so forming and formative whose language I live in?

Because the Night played in the afternoon (of an eclipse). "Language as primary environment" applied to re-reading letters (one's own and others) the decades interleaved on every surface to blur and redefine the living in & of perception's architecture.

Charm (in Latin *carmen*): song, verse . . . incantation. *Carmenta* (Car the wise), a Roman divinatory goddess, invented the fifteen-letter Latin alphabet, though more likely the root of charm is *canere* (Latin "to sing"). English borrowed directly from the French *charme*, appearing first in 1300 with the same meaning (song or incantation with occult powers). By the 15th century it referred to the power of women to fascinate or bewitch, something 20th century charm schools still hoped to produce (for a fee).

Eleven

on reading *An Inland Ferry*

The ordinary Story is so often not ideal. — Susan Hicks Beach

getting between extraction long delayed on presently
the other side of wrapped last curve into detail of attendance
stock subject something else changing towards
fell in on top of inarticulate view
anticipated double gaze *closed door*
non-understanding wrinkle me to iniquity will want to read
there impatiently a classification
standing outside her impulse to encounter *divulge*
for these eventualities got past conventionally put
the knowledge forward in far-away
enough to invent this listening
daylight down perpendicular aflame quite mechanically
without saying reached horizon undid undertaken turn
to compel convenient intervals recital of confidence
experience an end in, itself sometimes lost
sense of proportion punctual act
on three sides only round in imitation
written up "ins and outs" *very un-epic*
remembered enthusiasm passes into profile
beside glint of foreshortened characteristic
clearness and a thin veneer when he said goodbye

which is the alternative eastwards answer
strange if you haven't been asked in either life
diverting disengaged inspection of interval at a distance
territory *overheard* lifted it should go to shape and self-sufficing
one link between they call themselves shadows or go beyond a second visit
pleasure wedgewise instinctive lapse
into hers appreciation accommodated along it restlessness
sidepath succeeded her visit arrived
occasion for illumination of murmur
response removal turns aside
and later absorption alone listening beside inmost angle
with a drift beneath fingers to rest in such
an apprehension not mere absence
to call your work disconcerting across movement still
leaned against it nameless star with a whim might drop
other practised phrases untranslatable truant
call conception venture to be met
carried up and between in succession returned quickly
"'Don't say 'long ago'" . . . tinge of accurate above a long time thus
on the unsubstantial verge noiseless top of it
is never bored during, do you think?
inevitable amount of paper
every detail on the low sill her back to, half-opened
withdrew it knowledgeable, accumulating
vague inference to objective parted again
breathless at the junction an inkling *is* hard lines a tenth of metaphor
evening time beyond them sense of tree-framed talking (rain) for the use of it

presence forgotten

no messy explanations

went towards folded hands connect a sudden

bracketting of the words "woman" and "dignity"

for instance on a noon day coast

thrown aside some caprice no other outlet

through curtains voices chanting

"many words crowded on to one note"

and on, on stopped, broke forth again

how many hours? to sit the voices out . . . inarticulate observation

herself presently

noise broke in pieces "all-overish"

slanting in on their say-at-once threshold

river-side (the interrupting sentence of deranged postures)

place, which outline

no rurality to reason its razure

borderland yet its place in the box waterside reverse curve

into a notebook aloof from gesture

or their absence

on the ledge beside unconventionality *accomplishment of an impulse*

sensation alone further vantage aforesaid

ripple's surface a list of strangers charm

pre-arranged beneath the clarity

beforehand repeated in suspense

the beginning at last

hidden presently disclosed to view

Twelve

There are people still living (1947) who have seen opium pills on sale in large baskets in
Cambridge market place to comfort the victims of the Fenland agues.
— footnote in *The Journeys of Celia Fiennes*

Perhaps the reunion or similar event (memorial, funeral, wake) provides an
extreme example of the fold when twenty or (many) more years separate meetings
of those referred to as friends. Sweet expectation the deceased will walk through
that door to the microphone evaporates when the word (*death*) comes to mind.
This experience is combinatory, not definitively an echo, yet certainly a partial
grafting of the remembered "known" with an introduction of accrued difference.
The focus is sometimes clear but then a blurring commences, abrupt shift between
the degrees of recognition.

. . . they have one good thing in most parts of this principality (or County Palatine its
rather called) that at all cross wayes there are Posts with hands pointing to each road with
the names of the great town or market towns that it leads to, which does make up for the
length of miles that strangers may not loose their road and have it to goe back again . . .
(Signposts had been ordered by Statute in 1697.)

She writes that the house (Ronaldsway) "was already suffering from the creeping
approach of architectural tragedies" at least ten years before its demolition (in
1943) . . . an ancient house (Viking Ragnwalds-vagr) originating in a watch-tower
on a peninsula to the east of the bay (now) called Derby Haven. And so too such
phrasing is applied to the once-living: ". . . non-success . . . queer but quite
recognisable it is an ineradicable weed that gets hold of the soil of a family history;

once the seed of failure is sown, neither prayer and fasting, honest work, nor worldly devices seem potent to root it out."

To take nothing for granted, even hesitation. Glass, grains of sand . . . or water, electricity . . . words to pheromones. More than immediate, simultaneous, convey. "Life was suddenly stripped of its outskirts and seen as a personal lucidity." Figure eights turned inside out, aflame in the snow. "[Gaston] Bachelard felt that time is experienced not as a linear continuum but rhythmically, in durations (durées) of more or less intensity and activity as mind, body, people, and society interact." To embrace process (act and concept) relinquish fixation not experience (and by extension, memory). Of course there was more than one Henry.

She cites A.J. Butler ("The End of the Italian Renaissance," Vol. III of the *Cambridge Modern History*):

Biography became increasingly common; and just as ordered history takes the place of older chronicles, valuable in their way, and often charming in their artlessness, so the domestic records which had been frequent in Italian families pass into regular memoirs like those of Benvenuto Cellini, the spiritual father it may be said of all who have written autobiography . . . The kindred art of letter writing, reached, so far as modern vernaculars are concerned, as high a stage as ever it held.

While Butler seems to ignore Saint Augustine his reference to Cellini holds, but what of the 12th century's Raoul Glaber and Guibert of Nogent?

To represent in an unfamiliar context the working creativity of concerns seldom encountered in that different frame. As in two references, but the journey itself, making relocation (or transference) possible, seldom being acknowledged as an experience in and of itself more than a necessary interval between points. So, to scrutinize the means *and* act. (The intervening reality as "job" for those providing service in this example and how *their* hours are measured by rhythms of transit. Where location becomes release, accumulation, sometimes delay, may be shared by both passenger and employee.)

. . . the villa . . . turned out to be a 16th century, huge, converted farmhouse [close to the village of Palaia], *complete with enormous outdoor pool. It overlooks a valley, forested, in which wild boar and pheasants live . . . it was marvellously green and QUIET. . .* (Carrara, Italy, 21 March 77)

. . . The Carrarans are particularly hardworking and consequently, very well off in terms of the rest of the country. Of course, this is the Italian Riviera. Huge villas are to be seen everywhere and I just found out that the Medicis had a small palace here in Carrara (where I'm not sure). (Carrara, Italy, 28 March 77)

Oh, speaking of the villa, it was hit by lightning on Saturday night. We were all calmly sitting around the fire after dinner and there was a tremendous storm raging and suddenly a flash illuminated the sky like noon it was so bright and the electricity died. Most of the fuses in the fuse box literally DISINTEGRATED. The line was hit. Poor J is coping with that today. Had to go to the Energy Board and report it according to the neighbours. He'll be coming to Carrara tomorrow. It was an exciting experience. G was petrified. I don't know why the rest of us weren't too . . . And the peculiar thing is it was gloriously sunny the next day and so dry one would never have known there had been a storm . . . (Carrara, Italy, 8 May 77)

The weeping willows so close to the shore of an eighth summer create a solitary refuge. Sky just visible in shifting splinters of blue, bark of the huge branch rough but otherwise accommodating. Towels to cushion and books to explore became regular additions every afternoon. Sand castles, deserted, melted back into the waves.

The space of the box car, abandoned, or the silo (similarly so?) in the vast expanse offer an enclosed potential, a pause, once-acknowledged-shelter now contracting rather than expanding with possibilities. Would the act of depicting the interior of the pause be the abandonment or connection creativity challenges one to make? The ongoing multiplicity of site(s) and locations of vector continuously reframe position.

To enact the process of construct . . . both a dwelling and propulsion through . . . areas of varying intensities form as perceptual cascades. Transform transfer to the pulses where the folds' edges combine.

Act of breathing experienced as simultaneous extension and contraction, prolonged release though not as in opposite of "to hold onto." Difference in air temperature that inside the balloon ascending and that of the ether in which it rises. Sometimes the heat of submersion is more intense than desert surfacing between noon and too.

Thirteen

historical letters 10

"I" is only a convenient term for somebody who has no real being. — Virginia Woolf
Following the implied direction of possessions, environment is a room more specific a person. — Diane Ward

Description as a partial view — this side of the building visible presents itself as a form of re(a)d. Ruptures in the membranes of circumstances close by, successively overlapping . . . what is interaction? A mutual touching within the same instance. If the fall is "free" then the trajectory knows no bounds other than contact or its delay.

I enjoy travelling solo. There are problems, but they're not insurmountable. The Italian and Greek men are totally perplexed by single women going around the world & it seems to unnerve them that there are so many.

On Tuesday the Italian government, by a vote of 156-154, vetoed a bill legalizing abortion. It's saddening to say the least.

Athens is more expensive, harsher, more tired in every sense.

BUT, it is GREECE, goddammit it, it's Greece & it's the beginning of my trip & I'm thoroughly enjoying myself.   love, love, love   (Athens, Greece, 12 June 77)

"The medieval mason combined the skill of the modern contractor, engineer, and designer. The separation of the art of design from the knowledge of building is a post-medieval development. The design and construction of medieval buildings were rooted in the mason's craft."

Weight of snow becomes icicles in a temperature change. Evergreens deeper colour against winter morning. How temperature affects *sound*. Deer in the woods the train track interrupts. How a man looks when sleeping on his birthday morning. Seeming touch of darkness against dermis but ether sustains both our *day* and *night*. The sealing wax of earlier centuries a brittle membrane informed by touch, different from callous. "Public Guidance Systems" for orderly queues in the temporary train station adjacent to the one being replaced, now detonated.

"A strange effeminate age when men strive to imitate women in their apparell . . . on the other side, women would strive to be like men, viz., when they rode on horseback or in coaches weare plush caps like monteros, either full of ribbons or feathers, long periwigs which men used to weare, and riding coate of a red colour all bedaubed with lace which they call vests, and this habit was chiefly used by the ladies and maids of honour belonging to the Queen, brought in fashion about anno 1663, which they weare at this time at their being in Oxon."

To write a work structured not as an architectural blueprint but as if exploring an architectural surround (known or unknown?) length of a line or sentence concurrent with number of steps toward a wall, punctuation as door or window perhaps . . . to write as one would explore a city, so a map would produce routes of numerous lines of a poem or the range of sounds heard in a given setting.

Perhaps the summer when tent dresses fluttered in lime and hot pink swirls if there was a breeze I watched her sketching the sailboats and painted a single butterfly on my own cheek. The lobby represented "inside" surrounded by floor to ceiling plate glass windows (no curtains) with the single option of door. Waiting for grandmother's social exchange to give way to a girl's anticipation of lunch the delivery man appeared as a mobile distraction to the adults' conversation. Noon. The brightness moved into one's pores, though airconditioning terminated what should have been heat. He was a big man. The sound of glass breaking all around his trajectory through the expanse of window covered us all. Repeatedly shaking his head and arms he attempted to shed the shards adhering stubbornly. The superintendent appeared. No one thought the man should drive but he refused to be taken to hospital. Amazingly, there seemed to be no cuts as a result of this newly dangerous portal.

Fourteen

DEVELOPMENTAL DICTIONARY (from 1967 to circa 1982)

contact, proximity
prologue, introduction,
production (of facts) to prove
general statement
of fanciful conception
hostile
meant to instruct
change of circumstances
(especially of fortune)
condensed and forcible
a general truth drawn from
science or experience,
principle
rule of conduct
short pithy maxim
significantly
conduct or speech tending to
rebellion or breach of public order
diligent, persevering, painstaking
irritable
of good appearance
seemingly reasonable or probable
meant only for the initiated,

private, confidential
broken in spirit by a sense
of sin
faculty of knowing & reasoning
understanding
of, appealing to, requiring the
exercise of, intellect
aptitude for any special kind
of action
a mental power, e.g. the will, reason
seize wrongfully
practically wise, shrewd
keenness of perception, penetration
contrivance, device
deceitful practice
deny existence of,
imply or involve non-existence
of dull greyish green or blue
covered with bloom as of grapes
grasping, extortionate, predatory
postpone execution or exaction of
(sentence, obligation)
give temporary relief from (pain,
care) or to (sufferer)
same as above
revile, abuse
obedient, dutiful, servile, fawning

substitution of mild or vague
expression for harsh or blunt
(e.g. "queer" for "mad")
attribute, impute (to), consider
as belonging (to person or thing)
essentially different, diverse in
kind, without relation
keen discernment, penetration
open, frank, innocent, artless
erase, omit
belonging naturally, inherent, essential
understood, implied, existing, without
being stated
forcible, convincing
mark out, distinguish, indicate
act of acquiring, thing
acquired, welcome addition
walking from place to
place on one's business,
itinerant
boiling, exuberant
irregular, abnormal
sprouting, developing
foreign to (object to which it
is attached), not belonging,
(to matter in hand)
unsatisfactory to the mind

meagre
of the extreme north
(of the earth or a country)
inhabitant of
hard to understand
profound
(of literary composition, etc.)
ill constructed, crude, unpolished
rare white metallic element
highly resistant to heat &
action of acids
happening at nightfall
learnèd
repetition of same sound

contiguity induction chimerical inimical didactic vicissitude pithy maxim
aphorism portentously sedition sedulous irascible specious plausible esoteric
contrite intellect intellectual faculty usurp sagacious discernment artifice
contrivance negate glaucous rapacious respite retrieve vituperative obsequious
euphemism ascribe disparate acumen ingenuous expunge intrinsic tacit cogent
denote acquisition peripatetic ebullient anomalous pullulating extraneous
jejune hyperborean abstruse incondite tantalum acronychal erudite tautophony

Fifteen

I was returning solo to North America from Italy and flew in via New York . . . unable
to get on the last flight out of JFK on stand-by as the flight was full. (This was a long
time ago.) A young man was in the same situation. We started discussing what we'd
do. (The friend I usually stayed with in NY was away.) The man was a ballet dancer
and I still remember his name. He was based in Europe but he was en route to see his
brother, to whom something had happened. After talking to each other for about half
an hour he gazed at me intensely and asked me if we should share a hotel. "Unreality"
became the prevailing condition as of that moment because I, equally intense, replied
"yes." So we went into Manhattan and found a room at the hotel where his dance
company stayed (can't remember which one), went out for dinner, discussed
everything from our respective relationships (he was involved with a woman who was
a dancer in the same company) to living in Europe, and art and dance and poetry.
Then we went out in search of emergency supplies before heading back to the hotel in
our jet-lagged if excited state (our respective suitcases had gone on already, so we were
in need of such items as toothpaste and tooth brushes, et al). At one point I remember
thinking to myself that I was in a potentially dangerous situation because I knew
nothing about this man other than what he'd told me, and the fact that I was intensely
attracted to him. During the following hours all sense of linear time was lost. Daylight
reappeared. We went downstairs for coffee. I distinctly recall that we did not say the
words "good bye." We kissed and went off in different directions (I was confirmed on
an earlier flight than he was.) When I arrived his luggage was next to mine. I read the
destination address on the tag and I can only now recall that it was a street name I
knew. We've not met again.

As for a blind date, well, that's how I met *I*.

Sixteen

A culture is a tissue of exceptions, whose incoherence goes unnoticed by those involved in it . . . — from *The History of Private Life,* Volume 1

Is it possible to dream that one is awake in bed in the "present" night, trying to fall asleep? And why not think about what came before both the chicken and the egg on the day a national newspaper's deadline/headline announces that human clones are ready-to-go? [10 March 2001] (though some of us contend they're already in-the-making, if unconfirmed via the media.) Sound as rain on a tin roof, again, wanting to hear this yet another time and the touch of still-wet leaves in the heat, unfamiliar now. A Devon summer, astride a father's late afternoon shoulders (nothing to do with the tide in or out but the six-year-old facing the intensity of an uphill cliff ascent) the view a vertical articulation of shift.

The letter K as inflection-to-be, vector, framed within "the name." Alice de Romili was responsible for building Bolton Abbey, followed by the Fane of St. Kentigern circa 1180. Thomas Christian, vicar, was visited there (later Crosthwaite) by Thomas Gray, poet, a year and two before their deaths. Pastoral beauty *only* was commented upon. His (the vicar's) handwriting was beautiful, too. Somehow she introduces a Hector Poirot to Hercule and no one spotted him. Ewan pulled the wig aged six or seven (1820). He further designed the National Portrait Gallery. Left drawing on his gloves, Samuel died at Wimpole Street, leaving a depleted income. One does not detect the whether patterns of parental travels.

The stairs to the flat in rue Saint Paul spiral to a view of children playing at regular intervals in the schoolyard where bells demarcate the intensity and trailing off of many raised voices. How institutions in various countries choose these systems of sound to determine units of an educational delay, parcels of time repeatedly wrapped and unwrapped.

Writers between 1500 and 1650 used all of the marks of punctuation in use today, but with observable differences. Semicolons will be met with only rarely, colons far more than today. Question marks were used then as we use them, but also they were used where we use exclamation points. These last were latecomers, being almost unknown before 1650. Quotation marks were seldom utilized before 1600, and then rather to call attention to a phrase or a sententious expression than to mark direct quotation.

The time of day doesn't linger but fearless, his act of "playing" with a scorpion by the window, the sun intensifying its transparency so the internal organs within that form, curving to culminate in venomous tail, fascinate us, terrify me, as the scorpion, claws raised, repeatedly attempts to strike. A Mexican later told us that this tiny creature was one of the most dangerous of its kind. Still he smiled without fear. There were several more years later that shared the house on Via Ficola in their stubbornness to find dark places to sleep in the summer heat. These large, black relations appeared more fearsome than the Mexican one but the Italians maintained that no major damage would result, a "fact" to consider when facing one who contested that territory known to me as the kitchen. We advanced but despite its speed my aim (with the usually-friendly fireplace implement) proved surprisingly true.

When one has an hysterical Mafia-esque landlady threatening to oust you from your "home" at any moment, who grandly informs you that everything and anything happening in, on, or near the house she is so kindly allowing you to pay rent for is your responsibility and none of her concern, who interrupts you in the middle of your explaining what has happened to a waterpipe to ask you if you are keeping the house clean and isn't it nice of her not to ask you to leave this year for the month of August so a doctor who formerly took it for that month can stay there, whose husband was supposed to have returned your call, but of course never did, so you end up spending more thousands of lire to ask him what's to be done, at which point he tells you he's spoken to his brother who happens to be one of your neighbours and the brother confirmed all you've said, so yes, he supposes you can deduct the cost of repairs from the next month's rent: to have to contend with this kind of behaviour on a regular basis does tend to make one worry.

I think what I don't understand about your generation is that certain members of it went ahead with the Vietnam war having been through WWII. Anyway, the Battle of Britain proves that people are capable of greatness and that is something for any generation!

At any rate, we went to an isolated and very beautiful black pebble beach at Cinque Terre on Saturday (Five Lands — just north of La Spezia are five towns along the coast, accessible only by train, except for one of them, which can be reached by car. There is a path along the cliffs joining them and in other years we've walked to all five towns, which produce good wine and olive oil). Some people are camping there this summer, mostly Italian and German youths. One does not have to wear a bathing suit!!!!! It was so hot I spent half the time lying in the water and am now quite, quite dark, for me.
(Carrara, 12 August 80)

A compression of one's sense of time proportionate to concentration when looking at a work of art or listening to a musical composition. How the ring-shaped smell of bread rises to a roof-top terrace on what-was-then-a-Naxos morning. Twinge in the right arm where fractured in three places when one was eight years old. What happens in the vicinity of the left ovary is "new" in the current abode with an increased rent as-of-1-August.

"— *a great deal of drinking tea and playing whist, people forever to dinner, and occasionally a dance.*" *At the beginning of 1780 the whole party set off for London, being five days on the journey; and two days later 'Miss Curwen' was carried to school — its whereabouts unmentioned. The days ran on . . . Meanwhile Isabella Curwen was behaving impossibly . . . Bridget and Mary set off with the rebellious girl on the return journey to Cumberland (April 7th). [Jane, in the fashion of the day, never writes of anyone, even her brother, by a first name.]*

"Between a mutual growth is a soil."

Seventeen

historical letters 11

Today, many physicists believe that nothingness is the foundation of everything, not just the arena in which matter resides but the substrate from which matter is actually constructed. As physicists envision the universe now, everything that exists is ultimately just a complex enfolding of the underlying substrate of empty space. This vision presents the universe, as English physicist Paul Davies has summed it up, as "nothing but structured nothingness." — Margaret Wertheim in *The Los Angeles Times* (cited in *The Globe & Mail*, 28 March 2001)

By the way I heard or read someone of the same name saying that Mac Cormacks are known for always going beyond what is deemed possible. I thought it very exact.
— Shelby Matthews (17 Aug 2001)

ह

"Slept at Clea — called at Brayton — din'd at Netherall."

How the *unknown* becomes the *known* (process again) and sometimes becomes lost, misplaced, suppressed, *de-known*, subjectively and collectively, from culture to culture ... even difference is derived from moment to image to context to degree of perception. Now it is the unusual quiet that fills the airport (made to feel larger when emptied of traffic) even our voices drop, except those on the loudspeaker system, and when the occasional cellphone irritates stale afternoon air.

The only medieval instrument of its kind to survive, the gittern [this example 1280–1320], forerunner of the guitar and played with a plectrum, was given by Elizabeth I to her favourite, Dudley, Earl of Essex. Modified, it now resembles more a violin. An eventual antiquity of now + "now." The countryside at 300 km an hour. To take one's pleasure . . . to make one's pleasure . . . or to create pleasure. Each successive layer a fragment focussed on yet unintended in primary form. Grace of a single gaze accompanying disembodied hand your gesture on my return.

Ruemours the *vaporetti* change in cadence but only the fog touches with certainty. Form of writing in response to temporal silhouettes (hours of similar duration unfamiliar in their staggered verticality with exhaustion as a temporary [passing] flat line). "Telling the bees" an act of recognition of (implied) interspecies communciation. Is it because their work so benefits our enjoyment? And what if the hive doesn't accept the new owner (following the deceased)?

Dimensions that exist but which we're unaware of, curl, the statement's alignments curved commentary. "Clouds with vertical development" pilot speak for source of turbulence. When attunement exists with another (absent) set of coordinates tension increases proportionately with those present. In the 14th century the English language replaced French "at the tables of the aristocracy."

(On) Sunday we decided to go to the Carnival in Viareggio down the coast. (It's the capital of the Italian Riviera tourist towns and the Carnival is quite large and happens once a year. . . .

all the huge (some 20 ft. tall) floats were of a political nature . . . the best was an enormous one depicting Berlinguer and Andreotti as Adam and Eve in the Garden of Eden. The Pope stood above blessing first one, then the other (the whole float had moving parts), while the snake writhed between them and Andreotti, as Eve, kept offering Berlinguer the apple (with "Governo" written on it), but never quite gave it to

66
ࢭ

*him. Birds of Paradise surrounded everyone and looked as if they were going to poop on
all concerned. It was MAGNIFICENT.*

*All the Italians were either dressed to the teeth or in costume and raucous singing was
heard everywhere, not to mention the atrocious brass bands and hilarious drum
majorettes who were so bad even the Italians laughed at them. But everyone had a
great time throwing confetti at everyone else and it was sunny and warm . . . The
Carnival runs for two successive weekends every February. As far as I know it has no
religious leanings (amazingly enough).* (Carrara, Italy, 7 February 78)

Perhaps the notion of lines, straight or otherwise, could be suspended so as to
consider the expansion, contraction, folding of that space where lines are imposed
on attempts to define the idea of time. (How ocean waves encounter beach in tides'
temporally apparent flux.)

67

Pogo and hoola-hoop Super-8-coverage of the childhood that included *Slinky* (when not in motion herself) those links would shift so effortlessly that it's no surprise gymnastics as singular was also turned to. Restless is as restful does. *Until* . . . clouds in the night sky might release precipitation . . . consider additional definitions throughout a lexicon. And add colour. Notions are porous. Each letter as monad for which alphabet works well?

Might not that shared sense of heightened attunement be an emotional version of a rarely explored dimension beyond the usual three? And what we refer to as a state or condition or experience we've named *love* is to act on the realization of extra dimensions. Or is it more akin to the scars our largest organ (the skin) provides evidence of? To be "in love" as one is "indoors." Each framing as one negotiates how the ongoing encounters open us.

When what *this* is is anything but . . . recall. *Carmen* the first opera listened to in full (a summer month but which recording?). Unfamiliar birdsong and Pulley's Bells in the snow a Lady Bug somnolent against the window screen and through this day. "The room with three windows" or the structure around the frames containing panes of glass. What we live without.

Each footstep a separate contact with heat penetrating the body from all directions until we become a part of it, a temporary insistence of climate's production. Pineapple's ripening scent fills a porosity adjacent banana, yellow. In the darkness fall the stars realigned for spinning differently within two "I"s sharing the verb *to see*.

Eighteen

historical letters 12
(no)thing (rien) which in Old French designates both the thing and its verbal negation;
there could be no more apt term to signify prohibition against the name.
— Alexandre Leupin
The days were long because so much of them were night. — Gertrude Stein

A particular letter is missing. Specifically, a key letter is missing, removed for safety
and now in limbo, testing my non-relation to investment. Since virtually all other
aspects have been brought to scrutiny this poses a surprise (unhappily). Which kiss
was it, or which intensity reinforced by memory, when the moment exceeds time,
simultaneously expands and contracts space? Knocked sideways and winded the
fragility enters strength as a series of accumulations. "The spellings of course are
variable and numerous." She employs "performance" in an extraordinarily
contemporary sense. "The prefix Mac was only given to those whose mother was
the daughter of a Celtic landowner." Raven's Isle. Not many of the letters are
precisely dated.

Burgeoning peonies heavy in garden after garden, full blown they collapse
voluptuously, sometimes into the shade of a Russian olive or next to a rose's thorn.
As early as the 13th century merchants had their country houses in Whitechapel. To
work across these veins is to emphasize how facts define a life; certain lines on a face
might relate to a series of events involving specific persons.

Waking in the early morning to the penetrating sound of rain filling Cape Town
streets, grounds, mouths, and the sea, above this sound a roof intact, tympanum.

Brief respite, dry noon. Missive now reinserted in top (middle) inner drawer of 18th century desk. Hester Bateman (1708–94) the lone woman listed in the goldsmiths' biographical appendix, registered her first mark in 1761 and expanded her business "into what was probably one of the largest in London." Advised to wear no jewelry of any kind when in South Africa. Platinum, discovered as early as the 17th century was not used extensively until relatively recently (its separate hallmark was introduced in 1975). The sound of the nightingale in Verona's darkness. A lion trap's seemingly small dimensions in Matjisfontein. An agreement was come to in 1703 which confirmed to the Manx *Their ancient customary estates of Inheritance in their respective Tenements, descendable from Ancester to Heir according to the Laws and Customs of the Isle.*

On to the border the next day . . . finally arrived in Istanbul at 6 p.m. A group of us found a nice hotel right near the famous Blue Mosque (the only one in the world with 6 minarets). The hotel is also around the corner from Topkapi Palace & is directly across from Santa Sofia Church and right down the street from a very large underground cistern, built around 500 A.D. (554 I think), which was used for storing water in case of siege. You can walk right down into it.

. . . I must say that Topkapi Palace is one of the most amazing things I have ever seen. The famous dagger is indeed breathtaking, as are all the jewels and jewelled articles in the collection. The thrones are unbelievable, the manuscripts are gorgeous, the silk tapestries, pillows & covers all embroidered & encrusted with pearls, rubies, emeralds, (oh the emeralds) are exquisite and awesome in their size. Turkish tiles are beautiful. There is a fine collection of Chinese porcelain and Turkish glass. I really could go on forever . . . In the gardens are two highly unusual trees. There is a breed of coniferous here that is quite common & what had been done was to plant one of these and then

somehow graft a deciduous with it. The branches of the deciduous broke through the bark of the other, giving the impression of a hybrid!

The Blue Mosque is one of the most inspiring places of worship I've seen. From the outside it is grey & gargantuan but inside its height and the blue tiles which cover the walls & domed ceilings are most impressive. Lovely ancient Eastern rugs run wall to wall on the floor (one must remove one's shoes).

. . . Today we returned to Topkapi . . . and saw the Harem, which was almost a separate community in its day (it was used from the 16th century to 1850), [i.e.] separate from the palace. Consisting of 400 rooms, it housed 500 women & 162 children. Some of the rooms had been fully restored & were indeed sumptuous, almost to the point of being gaudy.

After lunch we went to the Mosaic Museum where there were wonderfully well preserved Mosaics dating mostly from the 5th–7th century A.D., (a few from the 11th). The most impressive was the floor of the Great Palace. (The museum itself is in the ruins of this palace.) (Naxos, Greece, 4–7 May 76)

Is it the proximity of so many palms to the beach that produces unease? No sunlight penetrated the Caribbean waves at such an hour, no other imprints in the sand soon to be found in folds unaccustomed to planned granular invasion. An inability remains to concur with Romaine Brooks's statement "I fear those shadows most that start from my own feet." To implexify is not "to sleeve a two" (twist or unfold [silk thread] so subtle that it is difficult to untwist it). In England in the 18th century some 27 percent of urban larceny cases involved clothing.

Fletcher's brother Edward, editor of *Blackstone's Commentaries on the Laws of England* published Stephen Barney's *Minutes of the Proceedings of the Court Martial*, not in an attempt to defend the mutineer but to inform the public of the reasons for such an extreme action. From Coleridge's entry in a notebook (1795–98) "Adventures of Christian the Mutineer" to Elliot's arrival in England in August 1923 an indeterminate affair. A photograph of Elliot (the great-grandson from Pitcairn) was taken in front of Morland Close, Fletcher's home. The "directive shade" of Wordsworth indeed, as one Person from Porlock would know.

No deep friendships were established before the teens, but cousins were sister substitutes on a summer basis. Jumping from the cottage roof into the dark towards the lake, remember to cross one's legs and close the mouth on height(end) black, a splash, grip of temperature both directions stars and perhaps that moon. An uninhabited island's moss so soft it required no other adjective to sensuality.

Giuseppe Marco Antonio Baretti's phrase-book (1775) contains a set of dialogues in Italian with English translations, between for example, "the bed and the alarm clock, Saturn and the Moon, snuff and its box." Even a dog and a cat argue fiercely over the then contemporary exhibition at the Royal Academy. All for the purposes of easy phraseology.

Glimpses absorbed of the household economy: sparsely furnished, sun-flooded rooms across a black and white stone floor to one of oak, and a table at which sat a charming man. To be preoccupied with "the pecuniary aspect of life" was considered "bourgeois." That latter's revenge was and *is* good living. In earlier days I inquired (with an equal measure of anxiety and frustration) why "we" did not appear in the biography, published in the year of my birth. Nothing offered by either parent ever relieved the twinned doubts until I read the book.

Nineteen

historical letters 13
If friendship is a parallel then love is its intersection —— a condition where the Is are crossed. —— from Quill Driver

. . . an intersection is "invariant," it can't be destroyed no matter how much the lines are twisted. —— John Briggs & F. David Peat

The folio catalogue printed in the tower included 23,837 entries ("only a facsimile and an incomplete original existed in the British Museum, the fullest belonging to the Bibliothèque Nationale"). Thirlstaine House was home to these manuscripts and library of Thomas Phillipps (some 50,000 volumes). Susan (then) Christian glimpsed one of the galleries while working at a bazaar "for some forgotten cause." The freehold became the property of Cheltenham College, the manuscripts and books sold privately to German and Belgian governments, and later at auction. The British Museum may (perhaps) still mourn for "lost opportunities."

Odd sense that certain women's handbags are designed solely to accommodate those who are right-handed. Pay more attention to such observations. Dense foliage outside what was then an office window. In the photograph two palm trees and one catalpa, in memory the nightly intensified scent of blossoms. Shift of perspective from hill to mountain when meaning left the *see* and came ashore. Reading silently to oneself a little acknowledged form of gravity. Emotions manifest in stutters, too. How we introduce time to space, referring to "nights" instead of simply to a nocturnal condition on an unspecified date.

Last night there was a fire below us, in the back of the drugstore. At 1.30 a.m. L came bounding in to wake us up, (we are completely at the other side of the building, very safe), we rushed downstairs, barely dressed, (I got my shoes for me 10 min. later when we were allowed upstairs again), 3 firetrucks were there, 4 police cars, reporters, very few spectators & clouds of smoke. Well, it was quite scary. The firemen were MARVELLOUS, so friendly, nice & EFFICIENT. There is no damage to any of our stuff as it was all on the other side. L's workroom floor needs fixing and the firemen had to break a couple of his windows but apart from that everything except the electricity is fine. We'll have power again tomorrow. Apparently the drugstore left too much garbage in the back & that's what caused the fire. (San Francisco, USA, 21 April 75)

What is "family" other than a condition of strategy? Each will encounters another. The dragon trees in Tenerife are of a "very great age." When their resin comes into contact with air the former turns red and coagulates, and it was this "dragon's blood" that was used in the Middle Ages to "cure" leprosy. The trees themselves are members of the lily family, as is the distant Joshua tree (Yucca brevifolia). John Christian Curwen apparently planted most of those millions of trees that were in lush evidence in Cumberland in 1864, thirty-eight years after his death, by which time Belle Isle was similarly a forest of imported "specimen trees." In a recent dream the importance of conveying unusually-formed keys and removing strips of paper (with text?) from my throat before freefalling, only to regain the body several times . . . some preface to the bibliography death might make of a life after its living.

1 September 1993 — 18 September 2002

to be continued

Sources

Chambers, James. *The English House.* London: Thames Methuen, 1985.

Cherry, John. *Medieval Crafts: a book of days.* New York: Thames and Hudson Inc., 1993.

Christian, Glynn. *Fragile Paradise.* Sydney: Double Day, 1999.

—— *Fragile Paradise: The Discovery of Fletcher Christian, Bounty Mutineer.* Boston: Atlantic-Little, Brown and Company, 1982.

Dawson, Giles E. and Laetitia Kennedy-Skipton. *Elizabethan Handwriting 1500-1650.* Chichester: Phillimore & Co. Ltd., 1981.

Fowler, H.W. and F.G. Fowler, eds. *The Concise Oxford Dictionary of Current English* (Fifth Edition). Oxford: Oxford University Press, 1964.

Galleja, P.E. *Spanish for Travellers.* Toronto: Coles Publishing Company Limited, 1979.

Herrin, Judith, ed. *A Medieval Miscellany.* London: Weidenfeld & Nicholson, 1999.

Hicks Beach, Susan. *The Yesterdays Behind the Door.* Liverpool: Liverpool University Press, 1956.

—— *Cardinal of the Medici.* Cambridge: Cambridge University Press, 1937.

——*A Cotswold Family: Hicks and Hicks Beach.* London: William Heinemann, 1909.

—— *An Inland Ferry.* London: Smith, Elder & Co., 1902.

Kacirk, Jeffrey. *Forgotten English* (A 365-Day Calendar of Vanishing Vocabulary and Folklore). Rohnert Park: Pomegranate Communications, Inc., 2001.

McCaffery, Steve. *Seven Pages Missing Volume One: Selected Texts 1969-1999.* Toronto: Coach House Books, 2000.

McDowell, Colin, ed. *The Literary Companion to Fashion.* London: Sinclair-Stevenson, 1995.

Mills, Jane. *Womanwords: A Dictionary of Words About Women.* New York: Henry Holt and Company, 1993.

Morris, Christopher, ed. *The Journeys of Celia Fiennes.* London: The Cresset Press, 1947.

Sadler, Simon. *The Situationist City.* Cambridge: MIT Press, 1998.

Veyne, Paul, ed., Arthur Goldhammer, trans. *The History of Private Life: From Pagan Rome to Byzantium.* Cambridge: The Belknap Press of Harvard University Press, 1992.

Walker, P.M.B., ed. *Cambridge AIR and SPACE Dictionary.* Cambridge: Cambridge University Press, 1990.

Ward Thomas, Michael. *Horham Hall: A Short History.* Privately printed.

Spanish for Travellers [no author cited]. Lausanne: Editions Berlitz S.A., 1970.

About the Author

Karen Mac Cormack is the author of more than ten books of poetry, including *Quirks and Quillets* (1991), *Marine Snow* (1995), *The Tongue Moves Talk* (1997) and *At Issue* (2001). Her collaborations include *FIT TO PRINT* (1998) with Alan Halsey and most recently *From a Middle* (2002) with Steve McCaffery. Her work appears internationally. Of dual British/Canadian citizenship, she was born in Luanshya, Zambia and lives in Toronto.